I See Shapes

Alyssa Demitri

INFOMAX
COMMON CORE
READERS

Rosen
Classroom™

New York

Published in 2013 by The Rosen Publishing Group, Inc.
29 East 21st Street, New York, NY 10010

Book Design: Michael Harmon

Photo Credits: Cover udaix/Shutterstock.com; p. 5 nikkytok/Shutterstock.com; p. 7 © iStockphoto.com/phototropic;
p. 9 Bobkeenan Photography/Shutterstock.com; p. 11 woodsy/Shutterstock.com;
p. 13 Rudchenko Liliia/Shutterstock.com; p. 15 Ambient Ideas/Shutterstock.com.

ISBN: 978-1-4488-8637-1
6-pack ISBN: 978-1-4488-8638-8

Manufactured in the United States of America

CPSIA Compliance Information: Batch #WS12RC: For further information contact Rosen Publishing, New York, New York at 1-800-237-9932.

Word Count: 24

Contents

I see a circle.

I see a square.

I see a rectangle.

I see a triangle.

I see a star.

13

I see an oval.

Words to Know

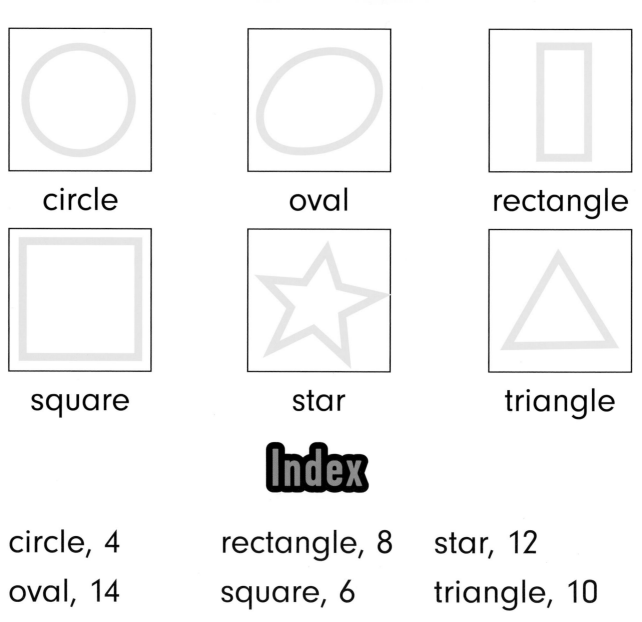

circle

oval

rectangle

square

star

triangle

Index

16